BELLWETHER MEDIA • MINNEAPOLIS, MN

Torque brims with excitement perfect for thrill-seekers of all kinds. Discover daring survival skills, explore uncharted worlds, and marvel at mighty engines and extreme sports. In *Torque* books, anything can happen. Are you ready?

This edition first published in 2025 by Bellwether Media, Inc.

Library of Congress Cataloging-in-Publication Data

LC record for Fairy Rings available at: https://lccn.loc.gov/2024009433

Editor: Rebecca Sabelko   Designer: Josh Brink

Printed in the United States of America, North Mankato, MN.

TABLE OF CONTENTS

A Picnic in the Meadow

Three sisters wander into a sunlit meadow. They are ready for a picnic among the flowers. Suddenly, one girl points to something in the grass. Mushrooms are growing in a perfect circle.

The two younger sisters rush inside the circle. It is the perfect place for their picnic! The oldest sister screams for them to get out. But it might be too late!

What Are Fairy Rings?

Fairy rings are circles of **fungi** that grow above and below ground. They are found in many parts of the world. They grow in grassy areas. They are also found in woodlands, often near trees.

Some fairy rings form small circles. Others can reach hundreds of feet across. They can also make other shapes.

THE FAIRY RING MUSHROOM

The most common fungus in fairy rings is the fairy ring or Scotch bonnet mushroom.

The easiest fairy rings to find often look like circles in grass. The circles can be dead and brown. They can also be deep green and **lush**.

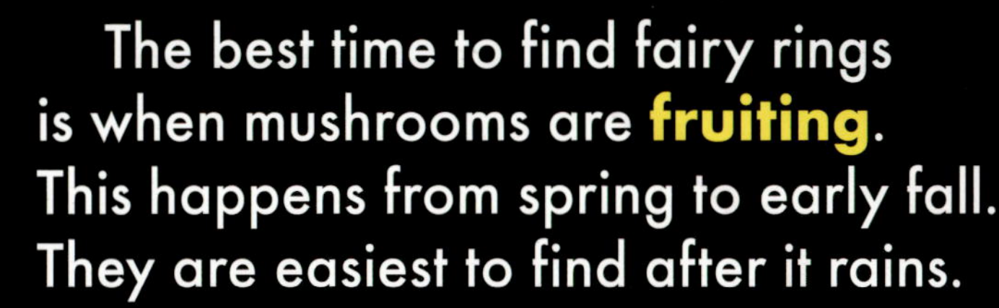

The best time to find fairy rings is when mushrooms are **fruiting**. This happens from spring to early fall. They are easiest to find after it rains.

Fairy Circles

Grass circles like fairy rings appear in deserts around the world. Nothing grows inside the circles. Some scientists think termites cause them. Others think the grass grows in this pattern to survive.

Beware the Circle

Long ago, many people were afraid of fairy rings. They believed **supernatural** beings made them. People in Austria once thought dragons burned the rings into the ground.

In Germany, fairy rings are called witches' rings. People believed witches danced in the rings to welcome spring on the night of April 30. People still honor this **tradition** each year.

A BIT OF LUCK

People in Wales were some of the few who thought fairy rings were good luck. They believed the rings helped nearby gardens grow.

people dressed as witches to welcome spring

Many European **cultures** believed fairy rings formed where fairies danced. The circles were doorways into fairy worlds. They were often considered bad luck. People who found themselves inside a fairy ring might get trapped in the fairy world. They may be forced to dance until they drop!

In Hawaii, fairy rings are named after the Menehune. These **mythological** people secretly build things at night.

1600s English art of fairies dancing

Curse of the Giant Toads

Who believed it? People in France

What did they believe? Giant toads appeared when someone purposefully entered a fairy ring.

street art of Menehune

In the 1600s and 1700s, scientists began to look beyond fairies and magic. Dry, dead grass is common in fairy rings. A popular **theory** was that lightning caused these marks.

William Withering was the first to believe that the cause of fairy rings was underground. In 1792, he found that the rings were caused by fungi.

World's Largest Fairy Ring

Size: Around 2,000 feet (610 meters) wide

Location: Belfort, France

Age: Around 700 years old

Fantastic Fungi

There are two main types of fairy ring fungi. Both begin underground. Free fungi grow in open meadows or lawns. They feed on rotten **organic matter** such as tree stumps and plant roots.

DEADLY FAIRY RINGS?

At least 60 types of mushrooms can form fairy rings. Some are edible. Others, like fly agaric, can be deadly!

The **mycelium** of a free fairy ring grows outward in a circle. Mushrooms may grow around its edges. Free fairy rings can grow up to 2 feet (0.6 meters) each year.

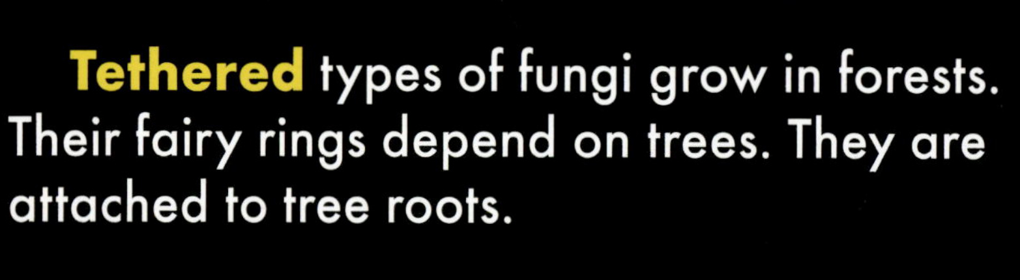

Tethered types of fungi grow in forests. Their fairy rings depend on trees. They are attached to tree roots.

The fungi and the trees help each other. The fungi deliver water and **nutrients** to the trees' roots. In return, the trees feed the fungi sugars. Tethered fairy rings cannot grow far beyond their tree's root system.

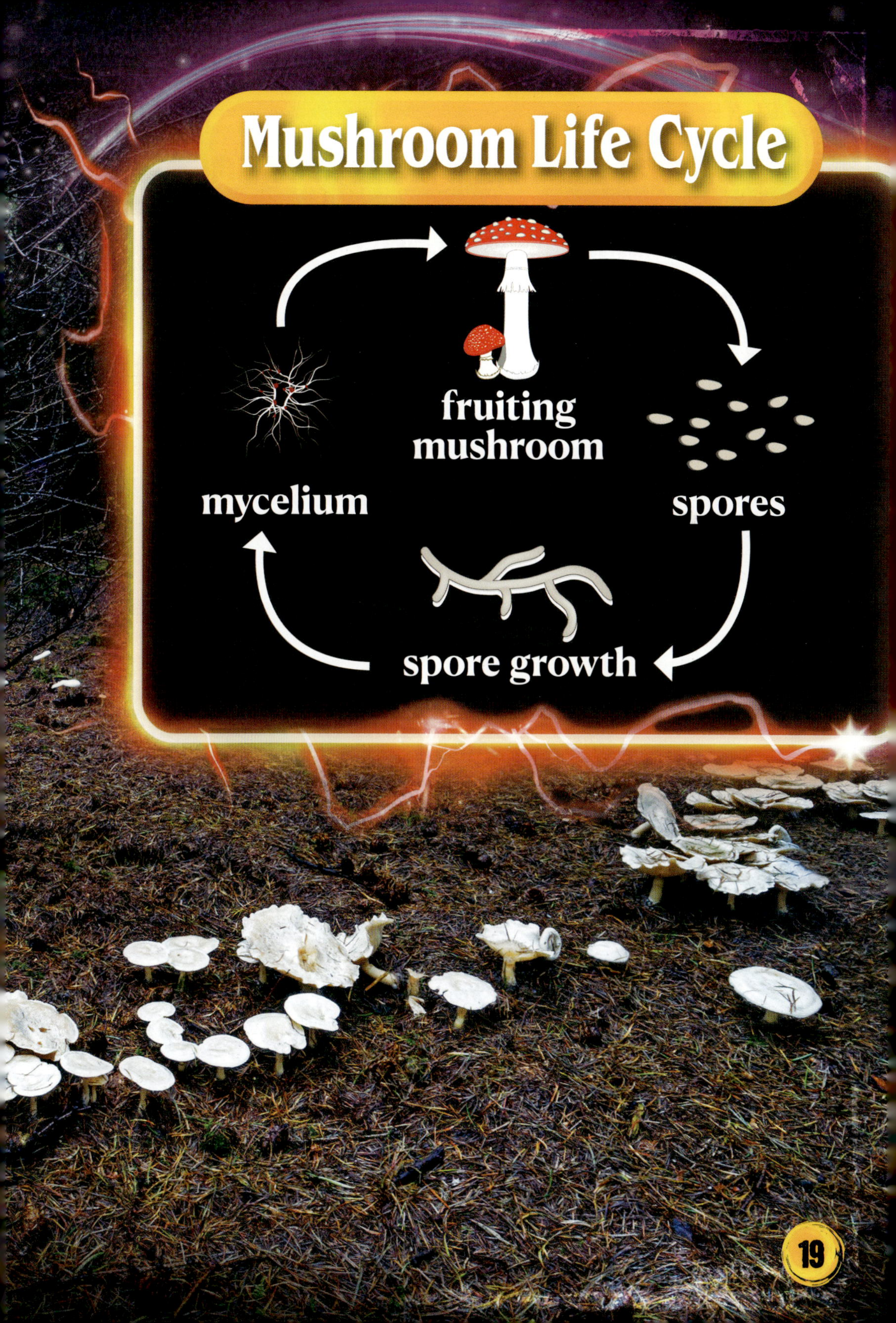
Mushroom Life Cycle
fruiting
mushroom
spores
spore growth
mycelium

Some types of fairy rings can be harmful to soil. But others are signs of healthy soil with a lot of organic matter. Tethered types help their trees grow well.

Tethered rings are more common. However, free rings are easier to spot on a stroll through a yard or park. Would you dare to enter?

GLOSSARY

cultures—societies that hold the same beliefs, arts, and ways of life

fruiting—bearing fruit; mushrooms are the fruiting bodies of fungi.

fungi—living things that are like plants but do not make food using sunlight; fungi feed on organic matter.

lush—covered in thick, healthy growth

mycelium—the mass of rootlike threads that form the part of a fungus that is usually underground or unseen

mythological—relating to ideas or stories of a particular group or culture; mythology usually includes beings with superhuman powers.

nutrients—substances that living things need to survive

organic matter—part of soil that is made up of dead plants or animals that have been broken down

supernatural—unable to be explained by nature or science

tethered—tied or connected to something

theory—an idea about how or why something happens; theories are educated guesses, not proven facts.

tradition—a custom, idea, or belief handed down from one generation to the next

TO LEARN MORE

AT THE LIBRARY

Boddy, Lynne. *Humongous Fungus*. New York, N.Y.: DK Publishing, 2021.

Troupe, Thomas Kingsley. *Fairies*. Minneapolis, Minn.: Bellwether Media, 2021.

Zimmermann, Laura K. *Mushroom Rain*. Ann Arbor, Mich.: Sleeping Bear Press, 2022.

ON THE WEB

FACTSURFER

Factsurfer.com gives you a safe, fun way to find more information.

1. Go to www.factsurfer.com
2. Enter "fairy rings" into the search box and click 🔍.
3. Select your book cover to see a list of related content.

INDEX

The images in this book are reproduced through the courtesy of: VitaSerendipity, front cover; FLPA/ Alamy, pp. 2-3, 22-24; Iakov Kalinin, pp. 4-5 (background); Diarmuid/ Alamy, pp. 4-5 (fairy ring); Novikov Alex, pp. 4-5 (grass foreground); Zoom Team, pp. 4-5 (shrub foreground); Irina Nedikova, pp. 4-5 (sisters); Matt Gibson, pp. 6-7; milart, p. 7 (mushroom); Susie Kerley/ Alamy, pp. 8-9; Felix Lipov, p. 9; Germany Images David Crossland/ Alamy, pp. 10-11; Chronicle/ Alamy, pp. 12-13; Jelger Herder/ Alamy, p. 13 (toad); Craig Ellenwood/ Alamy, p. 13 (street art); W. Bond/ Wiki Commons, p. 14; xpixel, p. 15; Ken Price Photography/ Alamy, pp. 16-17; Kichigin, p. 17 (mycelium); Juniors Bildarchiv GMbH/ Alamy, pp. 18-19; Designua, p. 19 (mushroom life cycle); Peter Barritt/ Alamy, pp. 20-21; shutternelke, back cover.